SIDDHPUR
PARIKRAMA

The Only Tirth for Mother's Salvation on Earth

Mrs. Geeta Sureshkmar Bhatt

Siddhpur Parikrama – In lyrical English by

© Surgeet

Mrs. Geeta Sureshkumar Bhatt

Gbhatt55@gmail.com

First Edition: 2014

Digital Print

ISBN: 1500621374
ISBN-13: 978-1500621377

Siddhpur Parikrama

The Only Tirth for Mother's Salvation on Earth

Geeta Sureshkumar Bhatt (Surgeet)

Siddhpur, my native place is situated in north Gujarat, India at the junction of two riversGanga and Saraswati. According to Rig Veda Siddhpur is the first home of Lord Narayan and Ma Laxmiji.The legend is that the great sage Dadhichi had donated his bones to God Indra at Siddhpur.Lord Kapil had created Sankhya Darshan Shatra and Kapil Gita to give salvation to his mother Ma devhuti.Since then Siddhpur is believed as the tirth for mother's Salvation. Siddhpur Parikrama is a tribute to my native. Geeta Bhatt (Surgeet)

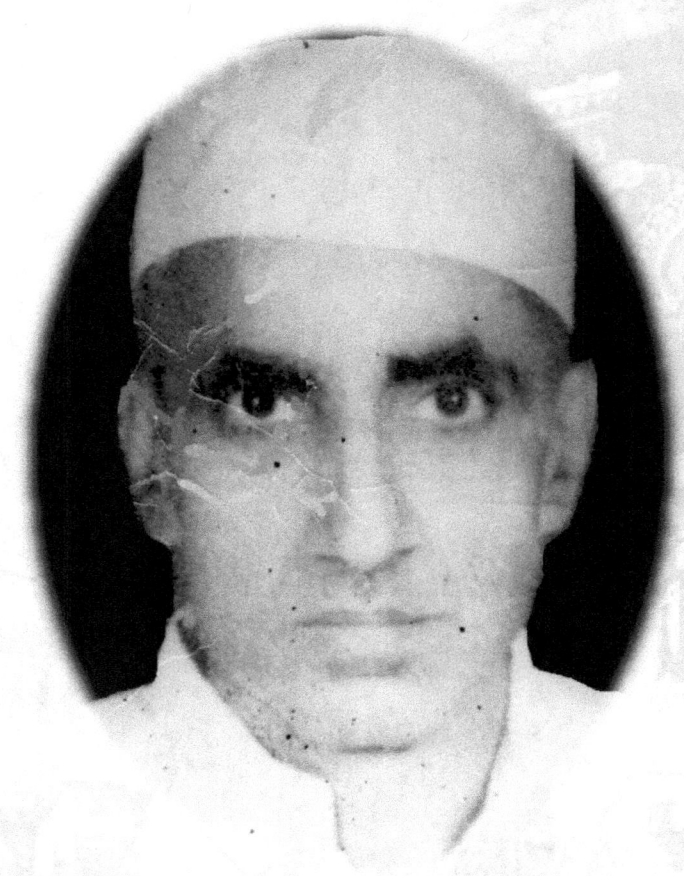

Dedicated to my Loving Father

Whose karm yagna inspires me as a light house in the life ocean

Speaking from the heart

"Ati Suvarnmayi Lanka Laxman mam Tannrochate

Janani Janmabhumishcha Swargadapi Gariyasi"

(Valmiki Ramayan)

Lord Ram in the Ramayan written by Rishi Valmiki tells Laxman above quoted words when they had victory over Golden Lanka of Rawan. The above verse says that though the Lanka is a Golden State and we had victory over it but I would not prefer to stay here as it could not be compared to our mother land Ayodhya in any way. What a longing for mother land!

A body of a person has to leave birth place for one or another reason but the fascination of a birth place can never be reduced an ounce. When a child borns and opens his eyes for the first time to see the world, he looks at parents, other family members, the roof of the house ,the garden of the house, the streets of the birth place, the friends and all living and non-living things make a universal panorama before his eyes. When a child starts learning and recognizing alphabets, vowels, consonants, relations, places, persons and day by day educates himself with his surroundings and worldly knowledge in schools, colleges, and Universities makes great impression on his mind. He cannot forget his first mates of the schools, the teachers who taught him a,b,c, d and 1,2,3. The persons and places play unforgettable roles in the memories of childhood and no man can forget them until the last breathe on the earth. Nothing can be said what happens after death and rebirth about the previous memories of the childhood.

The house where a child learns to walk, his baby steps and his tumbling down, his injuries on head, hands and legs, the staircase of the house, crowd of beloved buzzing around, fairs and festivals, occasions and celebrations with family and friends, laughters and cry knocked not only on the doors of ears but echoed on the doors of heart for the whole life and vivid shadows of pictures and videos flashed upon his inward eyes in hour of solitude, joy or depression. You could never know why and from where these past memories would flash upon your mind when you want to sleep at night after a totally tired whole day's work rushing to and fro for daily chorus. It may make you happy for a moment and it may make you full of grief at the other moment for the reason never known to anybody .No logic can be applied to it. And that's the reason in our religious traditions we have to pray God before going to bed and say sorry for the whole day's ungrateful deeds, is universally accepted.

My father would sit in the Padmasan even in bed, his posture remains erect, eyes are closed and his prayer would go on."What are you doing? Are you reciting any verses or doing prayer? What do you say to God every night?" That was my question. He tried to avoid answering it but my curiosity and persistent made him answer it. He told me," I am doing Manas-Parikrama of Siddhpur from our home situated at Brahmaniya pol's Nilkantheshwar Mahadev to Bindu Sarovar..Arvadeshwar Mahadev..Ashram of Guruji..Sahastrakala Mataji... and back to Nilkantheshwar Mahadev again."

Why did you do such a parikrama? What's the meaning of moving round and round to the different temples of the native?" His answer was," My whole day's exertion is overcome and I felt my energy re generated." I could understand nothing at that time as a child. Today I can comprehend it a little bit.

A tired body is prepared to rest but the mind, the heart, the inner soul is on the quest of energy continuosly.Unity in duality or duality in unity with Supreme God ! To do meditation one should have enough time and time is passing on in the daily routine. But the inner self, the unconscious spirit, the subconscious mind is longing for spiritual power and Energy always. The memories of deserted family members, parents, native land, home, streets and friends are on and on in the subconscious mind. My father had lost his father's shelter at a very young age. He had to leave his mother-my Grandma and young brothers and sisters at Siddhpur and he had to go to Mumbai to earn for economic stability of the family. He struggled in Mumbai a lot. His winning fight for the prosperity of the family and increasing burden of the responsibilities of younger brothers and sisters' education and marriages and social obligations made him toil hard. He successfully and devotedly performed his duties as a son, as a father as a social worker and as an exemplary human being. He was totally engrossed in the home, society, duties and religious work at Mumbai and Siddhpur.

But from the whole day's busy work and involvements into many social organizations he squeezed time for Manas Parikrama of Siddhpur every night before he slept. What a longing for birth place and thirst for the deserted mother and younger brothers and sisters! Every man is a child at heart. Had we ever understood his longing for his own deserted family members at that time? A person living in Mumbai, a great city full of entertainment and recreation with his own good financial condition could not enjoy life in Mumbai and missing his mother, relatives and friends, With MANAS PARIKRAMA of Siddhpur he perhaps sheltered in the lap of mother and mother land every night. I could not understand at that time.

Today I understand that while doing manas parikrama every night he might have been trying to be in the company of his family and friends, brothers and sisters and their company might have recharged him for the next day's morning. Whenever we heard him revealing anecdotes of his childhood in the Siddhpur we saw a twinkling sparkle in his eyes, a joyous jingle in his voice, a fulfilling contentment on his face and an ecstasy covering his whole existence. When we saw him in joyous mood we too became happy. Due to over burden of family responsibilities my father always remained busy .We find him always thinking over something or doing work seriously .To see him smiling and in pleasant mood was a rare sight for us hence whenever we find him in light mood and laughing that day became a festival day for us. His sincerity in nature and his honest devotion to the motherland crested with his dedicated services to all the needy people whoever comes to him for any kind of help. He was always ready to help anybody without considering his caste or social status. His thoughts are totally based on the Gandhian Philosophy. On every fifteenth of August, our Independence Day we are insisted to listen the Prime Minister' speech .On every twenty sixth January, our Republic Day we enjoyed national festival at home with sweets offered to God and listening the tales of freedom fighters .He always made us realize how much valuable Independence of India was gifted to our generation and how many martyrs had sacrificed their lives for this freedom of India. His talks were full of patriotic spirit and love for the country, the mother land India illustrious.

When I was in the first year of college he explained me my subject 'Indian Administration and Constitution' in such a beautiful way that I did not have to look at my text for the examination. He himself was not able to study after tenth due to his father's death but his command over English language was powerful. His knowledge of administration was admirable. His arbitration on legal issues was of justified even by lawyers and solicitors in the High court, Bombay.His administrative know how is full of executive smartness.His social relations were filling of warmth.His daily life was full of discipline and his bondage to the rules and regulations are unalterable. His writing was very nice due to the writing habits of old manual accounting books. His accuracy in work was appreciated everywhere .His attitude about culture and traditions was strict. His teachings and training attention towards girls in the home was more than the only boy-child, my elder brother in the home. He never compromised in the matter of principles. His future planning was full of safety for the family. His life-work was successful in every terms of the word. His active participation in the social life and his executive talents made his name and fame reach on the highest peak in the social groups.

His heart was longing to live life of a real Agnihotri Brahmin by doing daily religious rituals and worshipping God. But by doing nam jap of Lord Vishnu Sahashtranam and manas Parikrama ,he tries to console his soul. Perhaps searching unity in duality with God between worldly responsibilities and spiritual quest for self salvation was going on. This Manas Parikrama would be welcome by all the lovers of mother as Siddhpur is the only place on the earth for salvation of mother by the son. I hope that Siddhpur, a second kashi will remain a holy place till the sun and the moon regine.This is my tribute in words for the one and only Matru tirth Siddhpur from the depth of my heart.

Guess ...Since when have the trends of parikrama started? Since Lord Ganesh did parikrama of mother Parvati and father Mahadev? Or since kumar Kartikey did parikrama of the whole world riding on the peacock? Or since Lord Brahma did parikrama of Mahalingam of Mahadev riding on the swan up to the sky? Or since Lord Vishnu did Parikrama of Mahalingam of Mahadev in the swaroop of fish under the water of deep ocean? If we follow timeless theory to understand the ancient katha from puran ,Kumar Kartikey obeyed the words of parents' order and did parikrama of the earth thrice to win the bat while lord Ganesha followed the substance and meaning of the words of parents' order of doing parikrama of the earth thrice and thought that for a child the universe is rested under the feet of the parents so he did parikrama of Lord Shiva and Ma Parvati thrice and when the result was declared Lord Ganesh won the bat. Small eyes of Ganesha are a symbol of viewing at things very closely after pondering a lot. A sukshma Darshan! What is the meaning of this dev-lila (exemplary anecdotes for humans)? Feelings and intentions are greater than words and duty is greater than feelings. We know katha of puran. Once Brahmarishi Naradji wanted to know who is the great devotee of lord Narayan? Lord Narayan answered the curious question of Naradji in his own way .Naradji was told to do parikrama of the earth with a bowl full of oil in the hands and take care that not a single drop of oil should be dropped. When he came back after parikrama lord Narayan asked him,"How many times did you remember me? "Naradji told him that he was not able to remember him even once as his total attention was on the bowl full of oil. Lord saw him a farmer as his great devotee because he did nam Jap yagna thrice a day daily with all his daily work in the field and in the home.

Today a bread winner person is worrying and hurrying 24*7 for the comfort of his family and rotates like a top on the nail restlessly until he breathe his last. He had tied bandage of greed and selfishness for the wellbeing of his dependents and for the accumulation of property and prosperity .But don't you think he might be longing for self salvation by doing social services or by following any spiritual guru ?What is this Manas Parikrama a short-cut or smartness? No, not at all...

"Man avam manushyanam karan bhandhan moxayo"

A mind is the reason of bondage and a mind is a cause of salvation. If mind is pure and crystal clear you can enjoy Gangasnan (A BATHE IN THE HOLY RIVER GANGA)in your bath- tub. Hence a true devotees' mind is involved in God almost every moment inwardly; outwardly he may be found doing his worldly duties. The ancient Gujarati poet akho says,

'Tilak karta trepan gaya'

Means outer religious rituals cannot lead to the God or to the road to salvation.

What do people want to gain by doing parikrama or roaming round and round in quest of God or truth or something else? Lots of people do parikrama of mountains Himalaya, Girnar or Shetrunjay, Parikrama of rivers Ganga and Narmada, parikrama of lands -Lili parikrama of Vrundavan or parikrama of vraj by tumbling down their bodies in the sand of vraj VRAJ-RAJ? Many curious people leave their homes in the quest of finding secrets of the universe on the earth, in the great oceans and in the space. The astronauts, the pilots, the scientists, the pilgrims, sages, saints, travellers and wanderers in search of knowledge or something else roams around the universe. Why do they do parikrama of the universe like so many undefined flying objects in the space?

**"Yani kani cha papai Janmantar krutani cha
Tani sarvani nashyanti padikshana pade pade"**

When we do pradikshana or parikrama it is believed that we became sin free as it is in our shastra-holy books of Hindu religion .When we leave home, we leave all illusion and delusion. When we leave city or village we leave shelter and when we go to Mother Nature, we can have peace of mind as if we are in kailash Mansarovar. We do not have to find out our inner self, it comes naturally and automatically with God's grace. We become aware of uniqueness. Our unity with God in duality, sense of being a part of the whole universe, feelings of being one of the creations of the universe, feelings of being one of the great creation of the nature mother, sense of recognizing our own soul, sense of our lots of births and deaths and rebirths on this earth having different relatives and relations in every births and leaving them after every deaths .How many births and deaths have been taken by this soul? Nobody knows. We are not lucky as Arjun to have Lord Krishna to give us ultimate knowledge of the religion. The cycle of births and deaths create a web of religion and our deeds –Dharma and Karma but when we acquire knowledge the layer of illusion breaks, every soul is Arjun and roams for salvation. There is nothing new in this. History repeats itself. The new thing is how every soul finds his own way for salvation. The new thing is how every soul deposits his deeds and maintains co-ordination with his worldly duties, good virtues of honesty and devotional dedication to God. The new thing for every soul is how he remains in touch with almighty during every moments of his life span on the earth. The new thing is how he keeps repo with his inner self and the ultimate supreme power of God. The roots of God's dynasty are upward spread in the space and branches and trunks are spread on the earth. How can a man not knowing his inner self climb the staircase of various branches and trunks (by following different religions) reach to the original root and find God and salvation? Is it easy to go for the quest continuously with all worldly affairs, duties and responsibilities? But the way shown by my father inspires us even today to be honest in all our dealings with outer world and be innocent and pure like a child to God in our inner world.

My father was a kind person at heart. He never showed his back to duties towards persons of necessities. But his life remained busy for all the week's day. The feeling of a Brahmin (who remains busy in doing worship all the time) hurts him as for doing pooja and worshipping God, doing mantra-jap and performing religious rituals everyday he could not spare much time. While time was passing on and the river of life was pushing moments. So just like a farmer of ancient tale he remained strict to his own made rules and time table of worshipping God by doing Panch dev poojan in the morning and Manas Parikrama before sleep at night. What an exemplary management to follow! We cannot save father's wealth and prosperity, perhaps curse of Rishi

Bhragu punishes Brahmins even today about destroying property before it enriched the third generations. But we hope that we can preserve his cultural values of samskar. We can follow his intentions of doing well to others. We can enrich our inner self; we can do something for the family, society and country. We can avoid illusion and delusion of material prosperity and learn to keep things for self up to the necessity only and rest for the needy people by serving people. And let it be our Dharma Yagna Seva karma. Let have strength to put his ideals in the actions and deeds. This Siddhpur Parikrama is a tribute to my loving father with prayer to God to make his eternal journey towards HIM with dignity of great divine soul and let him make free from the cycle of births and deaths and give his soul rest in the lap of mother Parvati and Father Shiv peacefully forever.

Geeta Bhatt.
© *Surgeet*

Facebook : www.facebook.com/surgeet

Email me at : gbhatt55@gmail.com

Siddhpur Parikrama

Once a while you visit our Siddhpur Tirth (2)

Earth is our mother, protector and savior

India is a crown, Gujarat is a liver

Hey... Siddhpur is a lap of mother, have your peace of mind...Once...1

When you're far away, you long for mother's love

Come with me and visit, North Gujarat is the sight

Hey...Visualize yourself in Siddhpur; it's a holy place...Once...2

Let's know our land, do 'Manas Parikrama'

Lord's First home on earth, first Gruhasthashrama

Hey...Mother's moksha is gifted on, ma Saraswati's bank...Once...3

Creator of the Universe, Lord Brahma selected Siddhpur

Beginning of the world, He stayed at Siddhkhetra

Hey...Siddhpur is a land of Lord, Vedas state that...Once...4

Kardam son of Brahma, Born of mother Chhaya

Ordered by divine parents, to extend the human race

Hey...to create the human world, he came to Siddhpur ...once...5

Rishi Kardam did tap, years after years passed

To do job of creation, Human world on the earth

Hey... God came to Siddhpur and blessed Rishi Kardam...once...6

Creator of the universe, God shri Aadinarayan

Small particles of fire power, blessed India's holy land

Hey...to spread the message of karm, Selected Siddhpur ...once...**7**

Rishi Kardam asked God, to become his son

He requested Great Lord, to take the Avatar

Hey...To obey God's order Rishi, entered the Gruhasthashram...once...**8**

God's tears of joy created, Bindusarovar at Siddhpur

According to Hindu culture, matrutarpan is done here

Hey...Bindu Sarovar is mentioned, in the Rigveda...once...**9**

Great messenger of God, devotee Narad Rishi guided

Ordered the king of universe, great Manu and Shatrupa

Hey...Following lord's order, they came to Siddhkshetra...once...**10**

Manu was the king of, Whole Universe Brahmavart

His wife Shatrupa gave birth, to three daughters

Hey...For the weddings of daughters, they visited Siddhpur...once...**11**

Kanya Devhuti was given, to Maharshi Kardam

Ansuyaji was given, to Atri in Kanyadan

Hey...Atri and Ansuyaji were Parents of, Lord Dattatrey...once...**12**

Kardam and Devhuti, blessed with nine daughters

To be blessed with son, they did severe tap

Hey... God fulfills the promise, and Kapil Avtar was there...once...**13**

According to Hindu culture, matru tarpan is done here

Dadhichi Rishi donated, his bones to Indra Dev

Hey...For survival of his throne, the vajra was made...once ...**14**

Lord Kapil founded, Sankhya Darshan Shashtra

Mother Devhuti's salvation, by his son at Siddhpur

Hey...Since that day people carry out, matru shraddha here...Once...**15**

Beautiful is my native, ma Saraswati makes you Sin free

Do visit Matrutirth; be free from mother's debt

Hey... Unpaid parents debt becomes, cause of rebirth...once...**16**

Maharshi Kardam Adya Purush, Devhuti prakruti swaroop

Hindu rituals of marriage, were established by them

Hey...Rigveda describes Kardam- devhuti's married life...once...**17**

Ma Saraswati prayed, gods worshipped Narayan

Brahma and Shiv did pray, to activate human race

Hey... Brahma ordered Kardam to arrange weddings...once...**18**

Wedding was arranged, by Kardam Devhuti

Nine Kanyas were given, to nine Rushies

Hey... Siddhpur becomes the venue of, weddings of Rishies...once...**19**

Kapil Bhagavan has given, happiness to the universe

Imparted knowledge, People made doubt free

Hey...'Kapil Gita''s nine chapter, shown the 'Mukti Marg'...once...**20**

The Avtar of great anger, Tapomurti Durvasa

In his anger as usual, cursed MaLaxmiji

Hey...Laxmiji went to Kshrirsagar, to stay in her fury...once...**21**

The world became poor, dark in depression

To find out Ma Laxmiji, wandered here and there

Hey...All the gods then surrender to, Shriman Narayan...once...**22**

To find out Ma Laxmiji, the Gods with King Indra

Made a great army, devils do accompany

Hey...all were so poor and weak, without Mahalaxmiji...once...**23**

Chakshushmanvantar, a holy period of history

Yugapravartak Samudramanthan, done at that time

Hey...Gods and Devils all In search of nectar, churned ocean...once...**24**

Mountain Meru's sthambha and Vasuki's rope

Ma laxmiji's Avtar was gifted, by Kshirsagar

Hey...Laxmiji lived in Siddhpur with, Shriman NARAYAN ...once...**25**

Samudramanthan was done, poison came first of all

Nectar came at the number fourteen, from the ocean

Hey... Laxmiji brighten all with riches and, prosperity again...Once...**26**

Period of Chakshushmanvantaram, Vishwakarma was ordered

He created Prachi Madhav Swaroop of Vishnu, for Siddhpur

Hey...On the bank of Saraswati, made home for Ma Laxmiji...once...**27**

Siddhpur is developed, with their blessings forever

Ma Laxmiji is fascinated, and preferred Siddhpur

Hey...To please Ma Laxmiji Narayan, made their home here...once...**28**

Skandpuran's PraKshal khand, described that tale

Skandpuran is the creation, of sixth century

Hey...Siddhpur is well known as Shristhal, since sixth century...once...**29**

Before Kardam Rishi abode, many Saints stayed here

Gods- goddesses; Gandharva, Yaksha and Siddha

Hey...Charan -Pannag Stayed here with, Shri Prachi Madhav...once...**30**

Siddhpur is named as Siddhakshetra, since Vedas period

Siddhasthan and Siddhashram, names of Siddhpur

Hey...Sukhanagari name is mentioned, in the Vayu puran...once...**31**

Earth is holy mother, Prayagraj mentioned in Puran

Siddhkshetra is mentioned as holy, naval of Ma Pruthavi

Hey...Siddhpur is mentioned in the, Adwaitya Ramayan...once...**32**

Brahmdev did yagna, in the Siddhkshetra

Brahmandeshwar emerged, and takes Avtar

Hey...Brahmandeshwar Mahadev is, Kshetradhishthatrudev...once...**33**

Siddhpur is a land of, Maharshi Kardam Prajapati

Holy land of Siddhpur, Yagna Adhishthan bhumi

Hey...Shastra accepted Siddhpur, as Prajapati kshetra...once...**34**

Siddhpur is a land, where Kapil Muni born

Kapil Sankhyacharya, propagated knowledge

Hey...Abhedgyan of purush-prakruti, taught by Kapilmuni...once...**35**

Kailashvasi Mahadev, established in the Rudramahal

The land is considered, as holy as Kedarnath

Hey...Siddhpur is known even today, for great Rudramahal...once...**36**

Mahabharat puran describes, War of Kaurav- Pandavas

Dushashan was killed, by great worrier Bhimsen

Hey... He came to confess, at the bank of ma Saraswati...once...37

After killing Kauravas , drinking blood of Dushashan

Bhimsen bathe in Bindusarovar, worshipped Prachi Madhav

Hey...Pandavas visited Siddhpur to confess, brothers' killing...once...38

Ma Ganga papvimochini makes people sin free

Ma Ganga asked Hari, How to release her burden of sins

Hey...Lord Vishnu assured Ma gangaji, make her sin free...once...39

Lord told Ma Ganga, to visit Siddhpur Ma Saraswati

Lord Vishnu lives in Siddhpur, to purify as committed

Hey...Ma Ganga invited at Siddhpur, to be free from the curse...once...40

Ma Ganga with Ma Yamuna came to Siddhpur

On every Kartiki Purnima, tri-mata meets here

HEY...ma Ganga, Saraswati and Yamuna make, Triveni Sangam .once..41

Since ages long on the, Kartiki Purnima's fair

Devotees of Goddess, Visit Siddhpur every year

Hey... to purify body and mind, and to brighten their soul...once...42

Kartiki Purnima s'fair, well known in the world

Devotees from world, cities and villages of India

Hey... do visit the fair, enjoy heavenly freedom...once...**43**

When Krishna's elder brother, Baldev killed Sutpurani

Killing of Brahmin, considered a sinful act

Hey...Baldevji purify himself, in the Bindu sarovar...Once...**44**

All over India there are, four Bindu Sarovar

Siddhpur and Bhuvaneshwar, near Jagnnath

Hey... third is in the Kurukshetra, fourth the Himalaya...once...**45**

Mahabharat states, Pandavas visited Siddhkshetra

In their exile, they stayed at Siddhpur

Hey... History reveals truth, Gurjara of Iran settled here...Once...**46**

Around tenth century, Solanki rulers ruled

Siddharaj Jaysinh invited, Brahmins from Mathura

Hey...Muhammad Ghori destroyed town, on his way to Somanath.Once.**47**

Lord Parshuram worshipped, for his sins at Bindu sarovar

He did Matru shraddha, for his mother's moksha

Hey... Matrutarpan is an act of devotion at, Siddhpur...once...**48**

Historical Devbhumi is, my native place

Ma Saraswati's lap gives you, divine peace

Hey...Do visit Siddhpur and enjoy, heavenly pleasure...once...**49**

For father's moksha, three Gayajis are famous

Padgaya, Shirogaya, Nabhigaya is wellknown

Hey... Padgaya is known as Vishnuji's padkamal...once...**50**

Vishnuji put his charan on rakshash Gayasur

Naval is a source of, everybody's birth

Hey...Nabhigaya is at Bindu sarovar, Siddhpur is Matrutirth...once...**51**

At Shirogaya Vishnuji's charan, on the head of Gayasur

Shirogaya Brahmkapali is, at the bank of Ma Ganga

Hey...Bathe in Naradkund Badrikashram, do tarpan ...once...**52**

During eleventh century, the king of Gujarat

Mulraj Solanki great name of, solanki dynasty

Hey... killed his maternal uncle and, became the ruler ...once...**53**

Mularaj was a devotee and the bravest soldier

Felt guilty as he, murdered his uncle

Hey... to confess his guilt of murder, visited Siddhpur...once...**54**

He did charity a lot, and repented a lot

Performed Shraddha, prayed for mental peace

Hey...Came to Siddhpur , surrender to Ma Saraswati here...once...**55**

Siddhapur Siddhkshetra, Devshankar guruji is here

Did severe tapshcharya, at Arvadeshwar Mahadev

Hey...do visit Guruji's Ashram, to inspire you well...once...**56**

Holy shrine of Arvdeshwar, full of mango trees

Fruits flowers creepers, Natural beauty and peace

Hey...plants of medicines cure, your body and mind...once...**57**

Holy Pyramids are made, for yoga and meditation

Gurudev Dattatrey, Goga Maharaj regines

Hey...Miracles happen, for devotee full of faith...once...**58**

Yagna poojan nam-jap and kirtan worship

Rejuvinine your body and mind, in the Ashram

Hey...Libraries of Veda Upanishad, with Yagnashala here...once...**59**

Shri Devshankar Guruji, born on fifteenth of November

Eighteen eighty six, the Prestigious year for us

Hey.Knowledge of karmkand- astrology, from kashi Vidyalay.once.**60**

Completing duty at home, left home for Tapashcharya

Fifty years of meditation, aid spiritual guidance forever

Hey... Gurubapa is blessing everyone, in hours of need... once...**61**

Shankaracharya ji and Rang Avdhootji

Guru Golvarkar and Dongareji Maharaj

Hey...Great saints visit Ashrama, for darshan of Guruji...once...**62**

To be free from worries and tensions, Dhyan kutirs are made

Yoga and meditations, Satsang and gyan-charcha always

Hey.thousands of devotees visit Ashram, on Guru Purnima every year.once.**63**

One hundred thirty kilometer, away from Ahemadabad

Facilities of state transport, and a railway station

Hey...you can come by Unjha, Biliya, Kheralu road nearby...once...**64**

Guru Maharaj's father Shri Hargovindji Bhatt

Mother's name is shri Mahalaxmi matashri

Hey...Spiritual call made him leave samsar, for life of saint...once...**65**

Enter in the Devdwar, cross Saptarshi's seven gates

Near sacred Aoudumber tree, Guruji's holy shrine

Hey... Ashram has two parts, renovated for pilgrims...Once...**66**

Visit Arvdeshwar Mahadev, on the bank of ma Saraswati

Vishnu Sahashtranam gifted to guruji, by Ma Saraswati

Hey...blessings of Guruji, make your life worth...once...**67**

Siddhpur is a land of Siddha, great Saints visit Siddhpur

To pay tribute to mother and to do Matrushraddha

Hey...Siddhpur is known as Matru kashi in the world...once...**68**

Aadi Shankaracharya became, sanyasi for tap

Travelled all over India, to spread Hindu Religion

Hey... visited Siddhpur to perform Shraddh, of his mother...once...**69**

At Kadam wadi Bindu sarovar, Kardam performed Shraddha

Shri Nimbakacharyaji performed Shraddh, of his mother

Hey...Bell of victory donated with, unique design...once...**70**

Shri Madhavacharya known as Vayu Avtar

Performed Matru shraddha at Bindu sarovar

Hey...His Purvavatar was known as Panduputra Bhim...once...**71**

After the war of MahaBharat, Bhim visited Siddhpur

To purify himself from killing cousins in the yuddha

Hey...Do visit Siddhpur once in a life to pay tribute to mother ...once...**72**

Yudhisthir was the eldest, son of Panduraja

Bhim was the second, son in the number

Hey...Bhim established shraddh karmadhikar of every son...once...**73**

Bhim performed matrutarpan, at Bindu Sarovar

Great epic Mahabharat describes the tale

Hey...Bhim performed Kuntamas' Shraddha, at Siddhpur... once...**74**

Acharya shri Vijayindra, Satyapannagaji Maharaj

Did Tap for fifty years and stayed at Siddhpur

Hey...Performed Shraddha of mother, to be free from her debt...once...**75**

Ramanujacharya performed, Matrutarpan at Bindu Sarovar

On occasion of Koti kanyadan, established Ramanujadham

Hey...today the place is known as, Rajgopalacharya dham...once...**76**

Shri Ramanandacharya, Came Siddhpur for Matru Shraddha

Established Ramanujpith, to pay tribute to mother

Hey...Shri Raghuvarcharya came Siddhpur, to perfom Matru shraddha...**77**

To pay tribute to punyabhumi, Siddhpur Siddhkshetra

Raghuvaryacharya established, great vedant Institution

Hey..Verdant institute is well known, all over the world...once...**78**

Shrimad Vallabhacharyaji maharaj, visited Siddhpur

Performed Matrutarpan at Bindu Sarovar holy place

Hey...Recited Bhagavat Parayan to pay tribute to mother...once...**79**

Number seventy two Mahaprabhuji's bethak, at Siddhpur

Estblished by Shri Vallabhacharya, blessed byGod

Hey...Lord Dwarakadhish gave divya darshan at Siddhpur...once...**80**

The legend reveals with pride, Dwarkadhish's Pragatya Katha

Dwarakadhish emerged from, Bindu Sarovar after Vishnuyag yagn

Hey...Skand Puran's Arbud khand, describes Vishnu katha...once...**81**

This Dwarkadhish Swaroop, travelled and makes holy places

Established at Kankaroli, by Shri Vallabhacharya

Hey...Dwarakadhish pragatya katha granth, describes as well...once...**82**

Shri Sahajanand Maharaj, to be free from Bhakti Mata's debt

Performed Shraddh at Bindu Sarovar, Gifted copper Mahaptra

Hey...the tradition is followed by, true lovers of mother...once...**83**

All over India people do visit once, Himachal, Nepal Rajasthan

U.P., M.P. and Maharashtra, at least once in their life

Hey...Saint Mahatma Gandhi, Performed Matru shraddha here...once...**84**

Gayakwad of Baroda or Maisur Naresh,

Politicians, Artists or any professionals

Hey...Hindu Culture insists on, paying parents' debt...once...**85**

Gujarat Government is developing, preserving places

Siddhpur Matru tirth great Indian, Cultural Heritage

Hey...Indians cares for parents even after their death...once...**86**

Mahatma of Matru tirth, cannot be described in words

Wonders in Kaliyug happens, in Devbhumi Bharat

Hey...Blessings of mother shows you right path just have faith...once...**87**

Now let's do Manas Parikrama of, Siddhpur Siddhkshetra

Every night before you sleep, until you visit Siddhpur

Hey...Pay mother's debt and free from, cycle of birth and death...once...**88**

In the middle of the city, Holy shrine of the King

Shri Ghanshyamaji is here, Govind Madhav Swaroop

Hey... Come to crossroad, Siddhnathji calls you in Bawaji's wadi...once...**89**

When you turn back, Mox papal tree is there

Free yourself from, if Ghost or Goblin haunts you

Hey... holy water of Ma Saraswati, will bless you forever...once...**90**

Then go to Madhupawadi, Bhutnath is there forever

Hatkeswar's home is, on the way to welcome

Hey...Do realization of Ma Saraswati, purify your mind...Once...**91**

Find Kartikswami's temple, nectar in the well of Kailash

Ma Saraswati is there, bless you forever

Hey...Bow down to Lord Kartikey, blessed with strength...once...**92**

Find Ganapatray at Bhatona dele, With Riddhi and Siddhi

HE is obstacle destroyer, Leave your worries there

Hey...Hanumanji's silent zone in Vohrawad; don't make noise...once...**93**

If HE finds anything wrong, give you severe punishment

Break down your teeth; put you on the right path

Hey... Just start your work, and surrender to HIS wish...once...**94**

Turn to Desai's Mahad, Ma Bahucharaji is at thrown

Find Narmadeshwar Mahadev, at wrestler's ground

Hey... Find Great Siddhraj Sovereign; bless you forever...once...**95**

Thirty three corers' abode, Made for Eight thousand Saints

Visited top floor to watch prestigious Patan

Hey...To see Panihari with water pot, with every Sun rise...once...**96**

Law of nature is there, Mortal every Monuments

Great curse on King Rudreshwar, became fate

Hey...Aladdin was the cause, Pretext for destruction...once...**97**

Three and half whips, Reduced Rudramahal to ashes

Prestigious memorial, Immovable pillars are there

Hey...Symbol of great scripture, rare Architecture's work...once...**98**

Bow down to forefathers, feel pride in the world

Now look forward to Ma Harsiddhi, fulfill your wish

Hey... Ambli mata rush to you, whenever you call...Once...**99**

Find Ma Annapurna's abode, at Vedvade her Shrine

In the Vehverwad, Rudreshwar regines

Hey...Alaknath Supernatural fascinates, with miracle...once...**100**

Welcome to Patel lok's Mahad, Siddhnathji on the road

Meditate ma Dharamba, entrust to MaBrahmani

Hey...Khilatawade Ma Kanakeshwari, forgive us forever...once...**101**

Ma Ashapura is there, fulfilling every wish

Vahevarbhavani empire, Surrender to her

Hey...Ask for anything, and get it in a wink...Once...**102**

At Varahi's mahad find, ma Varahi's Avtar

Gogabapa omnipresent, Dattbapa protects

Hey...Don't forget to bow down to, Gogamaharaj's shrine...once...**103**

Shyamji Mandir beautiful finds Spiritual pleasure

Bhuvaneshwari Mataji, With Sonamata's Company

Hey...At Bhato's cross road Ma Hinglaj, welcomes pilgrims...once...**104**

Jadiyavir is your savior, Armour of your being

Turn back and salute, Viprawadi is HIS throne

Hey...Hanumanji's power and miracle, offer him laddu...once...**105**

Find Wonderful temple, Ma Jagadamba is there

Holy Navratri Poojan, Garaba's chanting is there

Hey...Worship Pataleshwar and Batuk Bhairav Maharaj...once...**106**

Salute Rokadiya Hanuman, at Hanuman gali's gate

Satyanarayan shines, Jagnath Mahadev protects

Hey...Lilabawa's glimpse makes our soul, rest in peace...once...**107**

Then turn to the right, Ma Varuni's glory bright

Her throne is on well, Surrender to miracles

Hey...Guru Maharaj's blessings, make you successful...Once...**108**

Khodiyarma's blessings shower, on Kharpada's chock

Govind-Madhav Rayaji blessed Siddhpur, under His shrine

Hey...Ma Laxmiji smiles, when you visit her home...once...**109**

TulajaBhavani's glory, VaruniMata on the road

In the deep street Upalisheri, Ma Fulwadi's rule

Hey...Listen divine music of anklets, feel very cool...once...**110**

Ashapuri fulfills wish, Kalyan Rayaji merciful

LaxmiNarayanji blesses, in the Laxmi pole

Hey...Permit new couple to live, divine married life...once...**111**

Enjoy fair and festival at, Shitalamata's nest

Get Baliyadada's blessings, salute Dudhalimal Boss

Hey...Make you disease free, cherish you as his own...once...**112**

At chhaththapad's mahad, Narmadeshwar regines

At the gate of Joshi's Khadki, Ma Brahmani protects

Hey... Don't forget to bow down, Satyanarayanji's shrine...once...**113**

Ranchodaji -Gopinathji present, at Radhakrishna's court

Panchmukhi Hanumanji's miracles, Surrender to his power

Hey...Do visit Gopalkrishna, Salute Ranchhodray...once...**114**

Do namjap yagna, and turn to brahmpol

Mahadevji is waiting, offer pujan and prayer

Hey ...Get down brahma pol's hill, turn back to muktidham...once...**115**

Mukti dham is Mokshaprad, for every living being

Ma Saraswati is waiting, now visit Bindu Sarovar

Hey...Bindu Sarovar is the place for, Matrugaya Shraddha...Once...**116**

Now you are at Bindu Tirth, bathe in the Gyan-vav

Dive in the depth, open doors of knowledge

Hey...Alpa Lake is wonderful, Do bathe feel yourself pure...once...**117**

Confess at the Bindu-Tirth, offer shraddha with faith

Pay tribute to your mother, Ma Saraswati blesses

Hey...Vedic traditions show you path of salvation...once...**118**

Crores' of sins, feelings of guilt wrong deeds

Get salvation at, Matru tirth Siddhpur

Hey...Forgiveness is committed here, by kind mother...once...**119**

Great son KapilMuni, Lord Vishnu's Avatar

Imparts knowledge and salvation to his mother

Hey...Darshan of Siddhkshetra, Supplicates for knowledge...once...**120**

Do MahaKali's Darshan, with Taramata's company

Mahadevji's Dehra one hundred and eight

Hey...Pray HIM to save your soul, and turn to Vegeshvar...once...**121**

Dadhichi Rushi's Home spread over six miles

Vateshwar Shiv imparted, Knowledge to Pandavas

Hey...they stayed for one year in the caves of Lord Shiv...once...**122**

Ask for compassion and, Sympathetic shelter

Have Bathe and purify, your body and mind

Hey...Ma Chamunda is calling you, Do parikrama there...once...**123**

Turn to Sahastrakala Mataji, Awaken flame of soul

Enjoy great fair on, Aaso sud ashtami

Hey...Brahmandnath Regines, feel yourself in heaven...once...**124**

Look forward to Hingalaj Mata, Arvadeshwar is there

Wonderful Ashram is there, Gurubapa's home

Hey...Do Chamkeshwar's pooja, and ask for anything...once...**125**

Valkeshwar Mahadev, on the bank of ma Saraswati

Laleshwar Chandramauleshwar, Present day and night

Hey...Before you cross Saraswati, bow down to Sahastrakala...once...**126**

Feel secure and protected, in your life's storms

From Pasuvadal's Pol, See Mata Sikotar

Hey...On Aaso sud Chhath, Join procession here...once...**127**

Tumble down your body and Ego, from VarakhaMuni's hill

Your body will be iron; don't have any doubt; trust

Hey...Khadaliya Hanuman's post is at, Rajpur's outskirts...once...**128**

Enter Siddhpur city From Pasuvadal's pol again

With Ganapatrayji's permission, Narmadeshwar's order

Hey...Ma Bhadrakali my kuldevi, fulfills every wishes...once...**129**

Your Parikrama is over, feel Heavenly shower

If you visit Chardham, Do Yatra of all Tirths

Hey...But if you miss SIDDHPUR, you lost Mothers' Blessings...once...**130**

God's blessings on earth, through parent's life is worth

Pitru Tirths are many, Mothers' home is one

Hey...Siddhpur is mothers' Kashi, The ultimate resting place...once...**131**

Writer and Author of over 23 Books including National Award Winner for Best Books

Spiritual Books:

Lyrical Translation of Sanskrit to Gujarati Language

1: Samanvayi Surgita (Best Book Award Winner 2012)
Lyrical Transalation of Shri Bhagavat Gita with Mahatmya

2: Ma Durga Saptashati
Lyrical Transaltion of Chandi Path with Complete Vidhi Vidhan

Lyrical Translation of Various Sholkas, Panchakam, Ashtakam, Dashakam, Bhujangam and Shtuti.

3. Shri Shiv Stotra Manjusha
Includes lyrical transalation of Suvarnamala, Shiv Stavraj, Shiv Mahimna, Shivanand Lehri, etc.

4. Shri Devi Stotra Ratna Munjusha
Includes Navratna Malaika, Anand Lehri, Mantra Matruka, Pushp Mala Stav, Das Maha Vidhya, etc.

5. Shri Vishnu Stotra Manjusha
Includes Vishu Sahastranam, Shri Hari Stuti, Bhujang Prayat, Vishnu Padadi Keshant Stotram, etc.

6. Shri Panchdev Stotra Manjusha
Includes Stuti on Lord Ganesha, Lord Ram, Lord Hanuman, Lord Surya Narayan and Gurudev

7. Matru Tirth Siddhpur Manas Parikrama
(Lyrical Form in English Hindi Gujarati with CD)
Includes Spiritual and Historical importance of the world's only place for salvation of Mother.

Indian Flame Series Books:

Lyrical Translation of Selected Sanskrit Verses in English Hindi Gujarati from Vedas, Purans, Upanishads, etc.

8. The Universal Vedic Art of Living (With Audio CD)

9. The Universal Vedic Wisdom

10. The Universal Vedic Mannerism

11. The Universal Vedic Management

12. The Universal Vedic Moral

13. The Universal Vedic Dharma (Religion)

14. The Universal Pancham Ved (Mahabharata)

More Books:

15. Krishna Harit Falak Uvach – THE BEST UNIQUE BOOK AWARD WINNER 2012
(Gujarati Poetries for Education Institutes)

16. Shabdo Mara Shishu Che-(General Interesting Gujarati Poetries)

17. Mara Shab Deh no Adhar – (Poetry Gujarati – A Journey from Shoka to Shloka)

18. Nrutya Natika Chaturdashi Gujarati – (2001 to 2014) Covering Various Topic of Social Awareness provided by Gujarat State Government)

19. Learn English in 108 days – A book on Spoken English Grammar Based Tele Education Course (Special - Grammar in Lyrics)

20. Indian Rhymes Based on Moral Education Vedic Culture.(For Primary Students)

21. Sharing Sangivini – Based on Shirmad Bhagvad Gita(blog-script)

22. Shri Manache Sloka-(Translated verses from Marathi to Hindi) written by Shri Samarth Swami Ramdas

23. Shri Manache sloka (Translated verses from Marathi to English) written by Shri Samarth Swami Ramdas

www.ingramcontent.com/pod-product-compliance
Lightning Source LLC
Chambersburg PA
CBHW051951280526
45789CB00009B/3257